# A Friend Like No Other

## Life Lessons from the Dogs We Love

HARVEST HOUSE PUBLISHERS

EUGENE, OREGON

*H. Norman Wright*

*paintings by* Jim Lamb

## A FRIEND LIKE NO OTHER

Copyright © 1999 by H. Norman Wright
Published by Harvest House Publishers
Eugene, Oregon 97402

ISBN 13: 978-0-7369-1847-3
ISBN 10: 0-7369-1847-7

**Jim Lamb**

Design and production by Koechel Peterson & Associates, Minneapolis, Minnesota

Answers to quiz in "What Else Would You Call It?"

| | | | | |
|---|---|---|---|---|
| 1. dog-eared | 2. doggone | 3. dog paddle | 4. dog-tired | 5. dogleg |
| 6. dogma | 7. dogtrot | 8. dogfight | 9. dog tag | 10. Dogpatch |

**Printed in China.**

07 08 09 10 11 12 13 / LP / 10 9 8 7 6 5 4 3 2

# CONTENTS

He is your friend, your partner, your defender, your dog.

You are his life, his love, his leader.

He will be yours, faithful and true, to the last beat of his heart.

You owe it to him to be worthy of such devotion.

Author Unknown

# HOW DOGS ENRICH OUR LIVES

CAN YOU IMAGINE YOUR LIFE WITHOUT A DOG? For most dog owners that's not a pleasant thought. While it's true that they take time, patience, and energy (did I mention patience?), they are worth whatever investment we put into them. Every day they are with us we find ourselves thankful for the way they touch our lives.

Dogs come in different shapes, sizes, colors, and temperaments. You may think your dog always existed as he is today, but most dogs are the result of purposeful breeding of several varieties to obtain selective qualities. In fact, dogs are represented by over four hundred breeds worldwide. Dogs have been bred to work, herd, protect, fight, and hunt. And there is variation within each ability. Some dogs hunt by sight, others by scent, and some point out wild game while others flush birds. Another example of different abilities shows up in the way dogs manage livestock. Some herding dogs round up strays. Others run around the herd to control it while some varieties stare down the biggest ram or bull. Matching the perfect dog to a specific need not only gives you a beloved pet, but a very valuable asset that will enrich your life.

And they touch our lives in many other ways. Arctic sled dogs often sleep with their masters to share warmth while Beagles can sniff out termites' presence in an infested house. Seizure alert dogs can warn their owners of impending seizures. Dogs are used for search and rescue, sentry duty, helping the disabled, and detecting drugs or bombs. Their abilities are truly remarkable.

In addition to evaluating specific characteristics, temperament is also unique to our dogs. Yes, personality assessment has now moved into the realm of canines! Incompatibility exists not just between humans, but between people and their dogs as well. They both share personality types. Bonnie Bergin's *Guide to Bringing Out the*

*A dog is not "almost human" and I know of no greater insult to the canine race than to describe it as such. The dog can do many things which man cannot do, never could do and never will do.*

JOHN HOLMES

*Best in Your Dog* contains a system based on social style. By using this system, it's possible to look at a dog and determine its personality type as either Analytical, Driver, Amiable, or Expressive. Which word describes your dog?

In his book *Why We Love the Dogs We Do*, Stanley Coren classifies dogs into seven different breed groups—Friendly, Protective, Independent, Self-assured, Consistent, Steady, and Clever. Going even further, he suggests dogs for extroverted and introverted people.

There's much to learn about dogs, but if you own a dog, you already know how much it can benefit your life. Once a dog enters your heart you are never the same again. A dog can, if you let it, teach you much about living as well as about yourself. Hopefully what is contained in these pages will either remind you of the value of a dog or open your eyes to the delights of participating in life with a canine friend.

But ask now the beasts,

and they shall teach thee!

THE BOOK OF JOB

# HOW TO TALK TO YOUR DOG

DO YOU TALK TO YOUR DOG? Of course you do. All of us who own dogs engage in conversation with them.

We greet our dogs when we arrive home and say good-bye when we leave. We ask them questions: "Are you hungry?" or "Do you want to go for a walk?" We even ask them questions they couldn't possibly answer: "Should I wear this suit or go casual?" or "Do you think it's going to stay warm or should I take a coat today?"

You're probably thinking, "I don't do that." Really? Listen to yourself for a while—you may be surprised.

For most of us, our language changes under different circumstances. We talk differently in formal situations than with family and friends. There's a special kind of language we use in talking with children as well as talking with dogs. We call this form of language *doggerel*. It's true! It's different. Do you know how it's different? Think about this: With adults we usually use ten to eleven words per sentence, but with dogs it's four.

When you talk to your dog, about 90 percent of your conversation will be about the present; after all, why bring up the past with your dog or anyone else for that matter? Also when you talk to your dog, you're 20 times more likely to repeat or rephrase statements than when talking to a person.

Most of what we say to dogs is of a social nature rather than items of information.

We also use higher tones, distort words and phrases to make them less formal, and place more emphasis on tone of voice. And finally, we (yes, we as people) tend to mimic the sounds our dogs make! So, when you catch yourself doing this, it's all right. You're a normal dog owner.

# WHAT ELSE WOULD YOU CALL IT?

Dogs have been around for so long they influence our vocabulary. In fact, without them what we say would be bland, even sterile.

Let's see how much you know about the usage of the word "dog" in our everyday speech. (The answers can be found on the copyright page in the front of the book.)

1. A book that's shabby and worn is . . . .

2. Another word for "darn" would be . . . .

3. An elementary form of swimming is called . . . .
   (If you didn't have this word, how would you describe it?)

4. When you're exhausted, you say you are . . . .

5. A stretch of land that bends is a . . . .(Golfers better know this.)

6. An established set of beliefs is called . . . .

7. A quick, easy-running gait is called a . . . .

8. A fiercely disputed contest is often referred to as a . . . .

9. A form of identification, especially used in the military, is a . . . .

10. Li'l Abner lived here . . . .

# SURVIVING PUPPYHOOD

WHAT DO PUPPIES DO? Puppies are great teachers. They teach you patience and consistency. They teach you to put things away, close doors, and never leave anything around you don't want chewed. They teach you to be on the alert, watch where you walk, and, before they're potty-trained, never walk through the house barefoot.

They teach you not to leave three dozen freshly baked cookies on the counter within reach of your puppy and then go outside for twenty minutes. If you do, he'll wolf it down. Ours did. That pile of flour, sugar, and (toxic to a dog) chocolate chips churned and fermented in his stomach all night. In the morning the vet taught *him* the meaning of an enema. Not a pretty sight.

Puppies frolic. They're mischievous…and they chew. They should come into the world with a sign on them "born to chew." If it moves, chew it. If it doesn't move, chew it. If it's soft, hard, pliable, brittle, dull, or bright, chew it! Your Ethan Allen Early American furniture could be modified to a new style—distressed!

Remember the first Christmas with your puppy? Especially remember the tree ornaments and how they tended to disappear? Fortunately, the green Christmas tree light bulb that our Golden Retriever ate wasn't that expensive—only 79 cents. It was *much* less expensive than his mistress' glasses he had chewed up two days before. It was that episode that helped me make the decision to take out a medical insurance policy on the pup. This little investment has paid off quite well.

*Somewhere my*
*doggie pulls and tugs*
*The fringes of*
*rebellious rugs,*
*Or with the*
*mischief of the pup*
*Chews all my shoes*
*and slippers up,*
*And when he's*
*done it to the core*
*With eyes all eager,*
*pleads for more.*
JOHN KENDRICK BANGS

*My little dog—a heartbeat at my feet.*

EDITH WHARTON

Remember that you'll survive puppyhood and its daily adventures and misadventures. We have time after time—including the episode with the "shrinking" garden hose. It wasn't that we had failed to buy a pre-shrunk hose… it was a nice, long, 50-foot hose. It started shrinking while we were away on vacation. A neighbor came over each day to feed our puppy and water the flowers. After the second day he was a bit puzzled. After the third day he was confused.

He said, "I could have sworn this hose was longer, but each day it seemed to be getting shorter." He was right. Every time he left, he also left the hose out. And as soon as the puppy saw it, he proceeded to chew off a six-foot hunk of hose and take off with it. It became shorter and shorter until I just threw it away.

I couldn't get upset at Sheffield, though. It wasn't his fault. He did what puppies are wired to do: If it's in sight, chew it up. That's the universal doggie rule. You can't change it, so don't try to fight it. Just put away the hose.

Properly trained,
a man can be dog's best friend.

CAREY FORD

## "YOU CAN STAY"

LAST WEEK A FRIEND CALLED saying he had a "precious" beagle puppy looking for a home. Say *puppy* to me and I lose all reason. I saw a small, droopy-eared creature with big brown eyes that said, "Love me." I didn't consider the headaches that come with new puppies. "We'll take him," I heard myself say.

Within forty-eight hours he had deprived me of sleep with all-night whimpering, shredded the draperies, and made a disaster of the carpet. Suddenly he didn't seem so "precious." He fell more into the category of an Egyptian plague.

"What am I going to do with you?" I said, staring into his brown-and-white face. He cocked his head at me. At once those eyes seemed to say, "Love me."

As I picked him up, I couldn't help but think how my experience with this pup was not so different from my interaction with people. Sometimes I reached out to them with a surge of emotion. But when I came in contact with their imperfections and discovered the nuisance side of their nature, I wanted to back away. Yet love, I reminded myself, meant taking the bad along with the good.

The puppy licked my nose. "All right," I told him. "You can stay."

—SUE MONK KIDD

*The great pleasure of a dog is that you may make a fool of yourself with him and not only will he not scold you but he will make a fool of himself too.*
SAMUEL BUTLER

There is no psychiatrist in the world like a puppy licking your face.

BEN WILLIAMS

13

God, give me by Your grace what You give to dogs by nature.

MECHTILDA OF MAGDEBERG

# THE NOSE KNOWS

NOSES COME IN VARIOUS SIZES AND SHAPES. Some are long and narrow, others are pug. Some seem to tilt up, others are plain and simple.

But for some dog owners, a dog's nose can be a source of embarrassment (not for the dog, but for them).

It's true, dogs sniff—constantly. They're smelling here, there, and everywhere. They have no boundaries when it comes to sniffing and smelling. It's just what they do!

I've heard people say to their dogs, "Stop sniffing there. Stop it, I say. Why do you always have to sniff everyone? Now, be a good dog."

Have you said this? Have you heard it from others? Have you ever imagined what a dog would say in reply to this if it could understand all this verbiage? Perhaps it would go something like this:

> My name is George. I'm a dog. Sometimes I hear people say they were born to shop. Well, I was born to sniff. I sniff and smell my way through life. I laugh when people tell me to "stop sniffing everything." They might as well tell me to stop breathing or panting. I was created to smell everything. And am I good at it! Oh, yes I am. Much better than humans. My sense of smell is at least a million times more acute than humans'. Why is that, you ask? My nasal region is much larger than humans'. I have fifty times the olfactory cells compared to humans. I'm olfactory gifted. They're olfactory challenged. Sure, my nose can get me in trouble at times. I use smell like they do to gather information. I discover life through my nose. I have sniffing power. That's why I can't keep my nose out of the trash can.

*Say something idiotic and nobody but a dog politely wags its tail.*
AUTHOR UNKNOWN

People read newspapers to bring themselves up to date on the local happenings. Well, so do we. Only we use our noses. When you take me on a walk, I have my favorite tree or hydrant. I go up and smell and think, "Ah ha, Rex has been here. So has Rosy, Sam, and (sniff, sniff) hmm, I don't recognize that one. And there's Prince! Haven't smelled him for days. Glad he's still around. I'll let them know I'm out today." And so I mark the spot too. It's the neighborhood doggy grapevine. It's my source of knowing who's around. So if you take me for a walk and you don't let me sniff all around…that's creating a SDCC (Socially Deprived Challenged Canine) and otherwise known as doggy abuse!

And remember there are many other times when my nose is a life saver. How many lives have been saved by dogs alerting their masters to a fire in the house? We've joined the police force because of our ability to sniff out drugs. Some of us have been trained to follow the scent of a person for over a hundred miles. Others can catch the scent of a person under water, buried cadavers, people buried under the snow, and those covered under tons of rubble such as in the Oklahoma City disaster and earthquakes. And I'm sure you know how much we are used for tracking wild game and assisting hunters.

Yes, we dogs sniff a lot. Be thankful. Encourage us to do what we've been created to do. Who knows, our sniffers may come in handy to help you.

# WHAT DO THEY KNOW
# THAT WE DON'T KNOW?
## (OR DO DOGS HAVE MORE SENSE THAN WE DO?)

DO DOGS THINK? What's going on in their minds as they lie there looking out the window or watching every move you make? Sure, the brain cells in a dog's brain work the same way ours do. And it's true that their brains contain most of the structures found in our brains. For example, vision is located at the back of the brain for both people and dogs.

But what goes on inside that head of theirs? Is there any conscious thought? Is there any rational process occurring? When they sit there with their eyes glazed over are they fantasizing about a juicy, sizzling steak, a romp in the woods, or leading *you* around with a leash and collar? When they sleep, dogs dream just like people. And little dogs dream more frequently than big dogs.

Do you ever wonder what's going on in your dog's mind when he's dreaming? You've seen a dog dream, haven't you? He falls asleep and his breathing becomes regular. His side moves gently up and down. And then . . . the dream begins. The breathing becomes shallow and irregular. Muscles twitch. Legs begin to quiver. Look closely and you'll see his eyes moving behind his closed eyelids. Then the sounds begin. Little yips, mournful groans or growls, or even whining may make you wonder: "What is going on in that dog's mind? I wish I could see a video of those dreams."

Perhaps we'll never know the answers to our questions about a dog's mind. But there is one thing we know for sure. Most of a dog's brain is used to create as many applications and variations of the verb "Let's eat" as possible. But now that I think about it, a lot of people I know are like that as well!

*One reason a dog is such a comfort when you're downcast is that he doesn't ask to know why.*

ANONYMOUS

# THINGS WE CAN LEARN FROM A DOG

Never pass up the opportunity to go for a joyride.

Allow the experience of fresh air and the wind in your face to be pure ecstasy.

When loved ones come home, always run to greet them.

When it's in your best interest, practice obedience.

Take naps and stretch before rising.

Run, romp, and play daily.

Eat with gusto and enthusiasm.

Be loyal.

Never pretend to be something you're not.

If what you want lies buried, dig until you find it.

When someone is having a bad day, be silent, sit close by, and nuzzle them gently.

Thrive on attention and let people touch you.

Avoid biting when a simple growl will do.

On hot days, drink lots of water and lay under a shady tree.

When you're happy, dance around and wag your entire body.

No matter how often you're scolded, don't buy into the guilt thing and pout . . . run right back and make friends.

Delight in the simple joy of a long walk.

# I'M NOT IMPRESSED

DOGS AREN'T IMPRESSED BY PEDIGREES. When a mutt meets a pure-bred with the name "Amber Britches from the Royal House of Winslow," he's not impressed. He couldn't care less. He's not intimidated nor does he behave differently. It just doesn't matter. It's no big deal.

How unlike us. We get hung up on titles, prestige, power, position, status, and money. We're uncomfortable around some people because of all those so-called "qualities." But not a dog. A dog simply doesn't have the hangups we humans have. Maybe it's good that he doesn't know how much he doesn't know. And even if he did know, it wouldn't matter if he knew. He accepts us for who we are regardless of our pedigree. What would it be like if we did the same?

*The reason a dog has so many friends is that he wags his tail instead of his tongue.*
ANONYMOUS

*The average dog is a nicer person than the average person.*

ANDREW A. ROONEY

23

# DO YOU HEAR WHAT THEY HEAR?

*A dog too, had he;*
*not for need,*
*But one to play with*
*and to feed;*
*Which would have*
*led him, if bereft*
*Of company or*
*friends, and left*
*Without a better guide.*
WILLIAM WORDSWORTH

DID YOU EVER WISH YOU COULD HEAR AS WELL AS YOUR DOG? Dogs can hear anything that has to do with food from three rooms away. And when you whisper to a family member, "Let's go for a walk by ourselves for a change," guess who appears in the blink of an eye. They are able to hear sounds at much higher tones than we do. Most people can't hear sounds above 20,000 cycles per second, but some dogs can hear them up to 45,000 cycles per second.

Since small dogs have smaller ears and resonance amplifies high sounds, they can hear higher tones than big dogs. But big, square-headed dogs can hear sub-sonic sounds. These are low-frequency sounds you and I are unable to hear. This is why Saint Bernards can hear faint sounds made by those trapped under snow. Some dogs can hear the almost undetectable sounds of the start of an avalanche and give advance warning. So, when your dog's ears go on alert, listen to what you can't hear. He could be telling you something. 🐾

Martin Luther said of his little dog Toelpel, "Ah, if I could only pray the way that dog looks at meat!"

24

# CONFESSIONS ARE GOOD FOR THE DOG OWNER

IT'S TIME TO 'FESS UP. (Yes, we're meddling!) It's time to get personal about you and your dog. There are certain questions that dog owners would probably like to avoid…but we're asking anyway.

We won't share your answers with anyone. You don't have to either, unless you want to. But you could ask other dog owners these questions and put them on the spot.

First, do you kiss your dog? That's right, kiss your dog! Do you? It's okay. One research study showed that 63 percent of dog owners kiss their dogs.

Do you allow your dog to kiss you? Only 51 percent did.

Let's look at the photos you have in your wallet. Would we find a picture of your dog there? It's okay. Market researcher Barry Sinrock found that 40 percent of those interviewed carry pictures of their dogs. And that's 20 times more frequent than pictures of their mothers-in-law!

Here's another revealing question. Do you ever talk to your dog over the phone or through your answering machine? Yes, that's right . . . the phone. Well, a third of those dog owners interviewed have admitted to doing this. (I have too.)

Did your dog fail obedience school or drop out? Of those that attended, thirty-three percent did.

Have you ever called your spouse by your dog's name? Thirty-eight percent 'fess up to this. And worse yet, 25 percent said they called their dog by their spouse's name! Guess who ended up in the doghouse that day?

Have you ever dressed up your dog with something like a scarf or ribbon? Eighty-six percent say yes.

And finally, is your dog named as a beneficiary in your will? If so, you're right there with an estimated one million Americans who have done the same. The only problem is that in most states pets cannot be left money or property in a will.

Yes . . . if we are honest we must admit to being, at times, a little foolish when it comes to our pets. But we can't help it—we love them! Somehow they cease to be "animals" and become instead treasured friends. No wonder we lavish affection and silliness upon them.

*Any woman who does not thoroughly enjoy tramping across the country on a clear frosty morning with a good gun and a pair of dogs does not know how to enjoy life.*

ANNIE OAKLEY

Dogs are not our whole life, but they make our lives whole.

ROGER CARAS

# SOUNDS YOU DON'T WANT
# TO HEAR FROM YOUR DOG

DOGS VARY IN THE SOUNDS THEY MAKE. Just go to a kennel or a local Humane Society shelter and listen. Most of the dogs are barking, but it sounds like the United Nations of Dogs with a wide variety of expressions. You will hear whining, yipping (in various octaves), light barking, intense barking, frantic crying, fierce growling—you name it, you'll hear it.

In your home you'll also hear a variety of sounds. Some dogs howl, others sing, most burp, and they all seem to sigh. They speak to get your attention, to warn you, to tell you they're hungry, to tell you they need to go out, to irritate you, and for no good reason at all! All of these you accept. You get used to them. But there are certain sounds you don't want to hear from your dog. Such as:

- The door of the refrigerator popping open at 2:00 A.M. If this happens, your dog's been watching too many commercials or perhaps he's been watching you.

- The sound of teeth being sharpened on wood. But you don't have any old lumber around your house! Don't worry. Those indentations on the leg of the table or the piano bench can be filled with wood putty. No one ought to notice them. If they do, simply smile and say, "It's the newest doggy decor."

- The sound of the lapping of water as your dog drinks on and on from his water dish. Only you're sitting there looking at his water dish. Then it hits you. As you rush into the bathroom, his head lifts from the toilet bowl, water streaming off his chin and he sees your look of disgust and hands on your hips. He stares at you (looking dumb) and his look says, "Hey, I'm a dog. What do you expect when you don't put the lid down?"

- The worst is no sound at all! Silence. You don't want to hear silence. Your dog usually isn't silent unless…(you fill it in. You know what trouble he's into now!).

*Let dogs delight to bark and bite, For God hath made them so.*
ISAAC WATTS

29

# HE COMFORTS ME

- A study of a twice-weekly dog visitation program in rest homes showed significant decreases in depression, anxiety, and confusion.

- Of 1000 elderly members of a Los Angeles health-maintenance organization, those who owned dogs sought medical care 20 percent less often than people without a pet.

- Animals give unconditional acceptance. They listen to the same story again and again, just as though it was the first time.

- Your heart rate tends to be lower when you sit quietly or read aloud in the presence of a friendly dog than when you do so alone.

- The survival rate for heart surgery patients is higher for those who have dogs in their home than those who don't. Those who own dogs tolerate stress better and have lower cholesterol and blood pressure levels.

- A study showed dogs were actually a better source of social support than spouses. Two hundred forty people participated in a stress study which showed that the participants' stress response was highest when spouses were present and lower when only their pets were there! Why? Well, it's probably because dogs are nonjudgmental or are perceived that way.

There is no faith which has never been broken, except that of a faithful dog.

KONRAD Z. LORENZ

# THE BOOK MY DOG
# HAS ALWAYS WANTED

*If you pick up a starving dog and make him prosperous, he will not bite you. This is the principal difference between a dog and man.*

MARK TWAIN

TAKE A TRIP TO YOUR LOCAL BOOKSTORE and ask for the section on dog books. It's there. It's large. It's full of books about dog breeds, training, breeding, etc. Some of the titles you'll see are *Do Dogs Have Feelings?, Dogs for Dummies, Puppies First Book, No Barking at the Table, Tales from the Bark Side,* and *The Dog I.Q. Test.*

Then I found it. The book my dog has always wanted: *Heeling the Canine Within: A Dog's Self-Help Companion* or *10 Stupid Things Dogs Do to Mess up Their Lives* written by Max and Scooter.

Some of the chapter titles in this self-help book are (this is really true!):

"Break the Cycle of Passive-Aggressive Chewing"

"Confront Feelings of Mixed-Breed Inadequacy"

"Stop Burying the Past (and digging it up again)"

"Apply the Principles of Power-Sniffing"

"Avoid Tennis-ball Dependency"

"Master the Seven Habits of a Highly Successful Dog"

I'm just waiting for the new onslaught of books to hit the market like *When the Owner Says No, I Feel Guilty, When Bad Things Happen to Good Dogs,* and *Owners Are from Mars, Dogs Are Called Pluto.*

## "COMING HOME"

I REMEMBER COMING HOME FROM THE NAVY AFTER WORLD WAR II. Home was so far out in the country that when we went hunting, we had to go toward town. We had moved there for my father's health when I was thirteen. We raised cattle and horses.

This is how I got Teddy, a big, black Scottish shepherd. Teddy was my dog, and he would do anything for me. He waited for me to come home from school. He slept beside me, and when I whispered he ran to me even if he was eating. At night, no one could get within half a mile without Teddy's permission. During those long summers in the fields I would only see the family at night. I did not know how to leave him. How do you explain to someone who loves you that you are leaving him and will not be chasing woodchucks with him tomorrow as always?

So, coming home from the navy that first time was something I can scarcely describe. The last bus stop was fourteen miles from the farm, but I knew every step of the way. Suddenly Teddy heard me and began his warning barking. Then I whistled—only once. The barking stopped. There was a yelp of recognition, and I knew that a big black form was hurtling toward me in the darkness. Almost immediately he was there in my arms. To this day, that is the best way I can explain what I mean by "coming home."

What comes home to me now is the eloquence with which that unforgettable memory speaks to me of God. If my dog, without any explanation, would love me and run to take me back after all that time, would not my God?

—DAVID REDDING

*Tis sweet to hear the*
*watch dogs' honest bark*
*Bay deep-mouthed*
*welcome as we draw*
*near home;*
*Tis sweet to know*
*there is an eye will mark*
*Our coming and look*
*brighter when we come.*

LORD BYRON

*A dog is the only thing on earth that loves you more than he loves himself.*

JOSH BILLINGS

# WHAT'S IN A NAME?

PARENTS TAKE GREAT CARE IN THE SELECTION OF A NAME for their son or daughter. So do dog owners. Chickens, sheep, cows, and goats aren't often given names, but if they are it doesn't take as much time selecting a name for them compared to the family dog. Some families have had major conflicts choosing the perfect name, and some have even had to resort to drawing a name out of a hat to make the final selection.

What does your dog's name signify? Who (or what) is your pooch named after? Why did you choose that particular name?

There are popular names, like Lassie, Snoopy, or Marmaduke, but they don't appear in the top listings. The top five dog names in the United States and England are:

| Males | Females |
|---|---|
| 1. Max | 1. Princess |
| 2. Rocky | 2. Lady |
| 3. Lucky | 3. Sandy |
| 4. Duke | 4. Sheila |
| 5. King | 5. Ginger |

If you're around other dog owners long enough you may end up thinking their dogs are named: "no," "stop that," or "be quiet!" Perhaps it's a good thing we don't know what our dogs would name us.

*The dog is the most faithful of animals and would be much esteemed were it not so common. Our Lord God has made his greatest gifts the commonest.*

MARTIN LUTHER

*He cannot be a gentleman which loveth not a dog.*

JOHN NORTH BROOKE

# I WANT TO BE CLOSE TO YOU

DOGS ARE INCURABLE BUSYBODIES. It's true. For one thing, they're eavesdroppers. They want to listen in on your conversations. And they have to be able to hear the sounds of other animals. They listen everywhere—around corners, down staircases, under tables, at the door, and near windows. They like to be involved in everything that is going on. They want to be let in on the latest gossip. It's a good thing they can't repeat what they hear us say. (Or can they?) We say things to them we wouldn't dare say in the presence of others.

They certainly are aware of us making sounds to them or to another person. But I wonder what they think when we drone on and on into that piece of plastic we hold up to our ear.

Sometimes you question their hearing ability when you give a command that's ignored. But then you realize it's still intact after you whisper words like "food," "let's eat," "treat," "get in the car," or "a cat's in the yard." They come running out of nowhere!

Dogs like to be able to see what's going on. They want to know where you are and what you're doing. They love to watch you when you're eating. They follow each slight movement of the hand as you cut the food and then bring it to your mouth. And when you say, "Stop watching me!" do you really expect them to stop?

Some dogs follow you everywhere you go. You walk into another room; in time, there's your dog checking everything out. You're in the bathtub and suddenly a wet black nose comes through the curtains sniffing, and then the head appears with an expression of "Well, would ya look at that!"

Can you stop him? Not really. He's just being a dog. Our pets accept us so readily for being the way we are. Perhaps we should do the same for them.

## DOGS TEACH US TO...

Take plenty of walks and naps.

Drink lots of water.

Don't think too much.

Never bite the hand that feeds you.

Bark when you feel like it.

Don't let people make you dress up.

Chase your tail.

Stop to smell the roses (and the grass, and the trees).

Make friends with everyone in the neighborhood.

Don't go for a run without your I.D.

Make people you love feel welcome when they come home.

# WAGS TO THE RESCUE

HEROES COME IN MANY SIZES. Their heroics are expressed in many ways. The response to help and save could come because of training, ingenuity, or even intuition. Sometimes we don't have an answer as to why dogs are heroic, but we have the results.

A number of years ago a group of dogs saved the children of Nome, Alaska from a deadly outbreak of diphtheria. Because of the severe January weather, an airborne delivery could not be made. An Anchorage doctor came up with the idea of sending a sled dog relay team from the nearest railroad stop, Nenona, to Nome.

They used twenty teams of Siberian Huskies, Malamutes, and their mushers. The dog teams kept on going through sixty below temperatures, hazardous ice floes, and zero visibility blizzards. Finally, the serum arrived. The dogs didn't know they had done anything heroic. They were just doing what they did best—pulling. What a wonderful example of helping others by just doing what came naturally to the very best of their ability.

In London, England a woman couldn't understand the strange behavior of her dog. He kept sniffing at a mole on her thigh. His persistent interest caused her husband to take her to the hospital. And it's a good thing he did. The mole was malignant. The early removal of it saved her life, thanks to her dog.

*Working there…guarding our precious bread corn from the varmints, I came to see what I would have been up against if I'd had it to do without the help of Old Yeller. …Also, look at all the fun I would have missed if I'd been alone, and how lonesome I would have been. I had to admit Papa had been right when he'd told me how bad I needed a dog.*

FRED GIPSON
OLD YELLER

*Be comforted, little dog, thou too in the Resurrection shall have a golden tail.*

MARTIN LUTHER

Can your dog dial 911? That's exactly what an Irish Setter named Lyric was trained to do. Her owner suffered from sleep apnea and asthma, a combination of conditions that could stop her breathing. Thus she spends the night attached to an oxygen machine.

One night the machine failure triggered an alarm. Lyric knocked the handset off the phone and pawed preset keys to 911. When the dispatcher answered the dog barked into the phone. This wasn't the first time Lyric went into action. Several weeks earlier Lyric dialed for help when her owner went into cardiac arrest.

Woodie, a collie mix from Cleveland, Ohio, saved his mistress' fiancé from drowning. Rae Ann and her fiancé, Ray, were walking in a forest preserve near a river when Ray said he'd like to take a good picture of the river. He asked Rae Ann to hold Woodie while he searched out the proper vantage point, but a few minutes later Woodie began to pull away from Rae Ann. The dog finally broke loose and ran off in the direction Ray had gone. Rae Ann ran after him. When she reached the dog on the top of a nearby cliff, she saw Ray lying at the bottom of the cliff, eighty feet below, face down in the shallow river. Woodie jumped off the cliff and pulled Ray's face out of the water. By the time Rae Ann reached the river, help had arrived. Woodie had broken his hip in his leap off the cliff. Ray was also badly injured, but he was alive, thanks to Woodie's courage. He became Ken-L Ration's Dog Hero of 1980.

*We give them the love we can spare, the time we can spare. In return dogs have given us their absolute all. It is without doubt the best deal man has ever made.*
ROGER CARAS

*No one appreciates the very special genius of your conversation as a dog does.*

CHRISTOPHER MORLEY

45

Beggar, a Saint Bernard, became his three-year-old master's hero when the little boy wandered away from his home in California. After a search was mounted, Boy Scouts found little Bobby wandering with the dog a mile away from home. Both boy and dog were dripping wet. When Bobby took off his wet clothes, the imprints of huge teeth prints were obvious on his body. Bobby told his rescuers that he had fallen into a nearby river. Beggar had jumped in and picked him up with her mouth, then carried him safely to shore.

Recollect that the Almighty, who gave the dog to be companion of our pleasures and our toils, hath invested him with a nature noble and incapable of deceit.

SIR WALTER SCOTT

# TRIBUTE TO A DOG

The one absolutely unselfish friend
that man can have in this selfish world,
the one that never deserts him,
the one that never proves
ungrateful or treacherous, is his dog.

A man's dog stands by him in prosperity and in poverty.
In health and in sickness.
He will sleep on the cold ground,
where the wintry winds blow and the snow drives fiercely,
if only he may be near his master's side.
He will kiss the hand that has no food to offer;
he will lick the wounds and sores that come
in encounter with the roughness of the world.

He guards the sleep of his pauper master
as if he were a prince.
When all other friends desert, he remains.
When riches take wing and reputation falls to pieces,
he is as consistent in his love as the sun in its
journey through the heavens.

SENATOR GEORGE VEST

*Acquiring a dog may be the only opportunity
a human ever has to choose a relative.*

MORDECAI SIEGAL

## BISHOP DOANE ON HIS DOG

I AM QUITE SURE he thinks that I am God—

Since He is God on whom each one depends

For life, and all things that His bounty sends—

My dear old dog, most constant of all friends;

Not quick to mind, but quicker far than I

To Him whom God I know and own; his eye,

Deep brown and liquid, watches for my nod;

He is more patient underneath the rod

Than I, when God His wise corrections sends.

He looks love at me, deep as words e'er spake;

And from me never crumb nor sup will take

But he wags thanks with his most vocal tail;

And when some crashing noise wakes all his fear,

He is content and quiet, if I am near,

Secure that my protection will prevail.

So, faithful, mindful, thankful, trustful, he

Tells me what I unto my God should be.

GEORGE WASHINGTON DOANE

## IN HONOR OF DOGS WE HAVE KNOWN

Some beautiful and moving tributes have been written about beloved dogs. Consider these:

> Here lies Dash, the Favourite Spaniel of Queen Victoria.
> By whose command this Memorial was Erected.
> He died on the 20 December, 1840 in his 9th year.
> His attachment was without selfishness,
> His playfulness was without malice,
> His fidelity without deceit.
> READER, if you would live beloved and die regretted,
> profit by the example of DASH.
>
> Queen Victoria

### Only a Dog

(Epitaph from a tombstone in a pet cemetery)

> Only a dog, but such love he gave
> Cannot have perished in the grave.
> So constant and faithful and true a heart
> Must in eternity have some part.
> And sometimes I fancy
> When I've crossed life's sea
> I'll find him waiting to welcome me.

*The one best place to bury a good dog is in the heart of his master.*

Ben Hur Lampman

## Lord Byron's Dog

A large monument was built at Newstead Abbey to honor Boatwain, Lord Byron's Newfoundland dog. Here is the inscription, written by Byron himself:

Near this spot

Are deposited the Remains of one

Who possessed Beauty

Without Vanity,

Strength without Insolence,

Courage without Ferocity,

And all the Virtues of Man

Without his Vices.

*I have sometimes thought of the final cause of dogs having such short lives and I am quite satisfied it is in compassion to the human race; for if we suffer so much in losing a dog after an acquaintance of ten or twelve years, what would it be if they were to live double that time?*

SIR WALTER SCOTT

## "THE GUEST OF THE MAESTRO"

WHAT HAPPENS WHEN A DOG INTERRUPTS A CONCERT? To answer that, come with me to a spring night in Lawrence, Kansas.

Take your seat in Hock Auditorium and behold the Leipzig Gewandhaus Orchestra—the oldest continually operating orchestra in the world. The greatest composers and conductors in history have directed this orchestra. It was playing in the days of Beethoven (some of the musicians have been replaced).

You watch as stately dressed Europeans take their seats on the stage. You listen as professionals carefully tune their instruments. The percussionist puts her ear to the kettle drum. A violinist plucks the nylon string. A clarinet player tightens the reed. And you sit a bit straighter as the lights dim and the tuning stops. The music is about to begin.

The conductor, dressed in tails, strides onto the stage, springs onto the podium, and gestures for the orchestra to rise. You and two thousand others applaud. The musicians take their seats, the maestro takes his position, and the audience holds its breath.

There is a second of silence between lightning and thunder. And there is a second of silence between the raising of the baton and the explosion of the music. But when it falls the heavens open and you are delightfully drenched in the downpour of Beethoven's Third Symphony.

*I talk to him when*
*I'm lonesome like, and*
*I'm sure he understands.*
*When he looks at me*
*so attentively, and gently*
*licks my hands;*
*Then he rubs his nose*
*on my tailored clothes, but*
*I never say naught thereat,*
*For the good Lord knows*
*I can buy more clothes,*
*but never a friend like that!*
W. DAYTON WEDGEFARTH

I care not for a man's religion whose dog . . .

is not the better for it.

ABRAHAM LINCOLN

Such was the power of that spring night in Lawrence, Kansas. That hot, spring night in Lawrence, Kansas. I mention the temperature so you'll understand why the doors were open. It was hot. Hoch Auditorium, a historic building, was not air-conditioned. Combine bright stage lights with formal dress and furious music, and the result is a heated orchestra. Outside doors on each side of the stage were left open in case of a breeze.

Enter, stage right, the dog. A brown, generic, Kansas dog. Not a mean dog. Not a mad dog. Just a curious dog. He passes between the double basses and makes his way through the second violins and into the cellos. His tail wags in beat with the music. As the dog passes between the players, they look at him, look at each other, and continue with the next measure.

The dog takes a liking to a certain cello. Perhaps it was the lateral passing of the bow. Maybe it was the eye-level view of the strings. Whatever it was, it caught the dog's attention and he stopped and watched. The cellist wasn't sure what to do. He'd never played before a canine audience. And music schools don't teach you what dog slobber might do to the lacquer of a sixteenth-century Guarneri cello. But the dog did nothing but watch for a moment and then move on.

Had he passed on through the orchestra, the music might have continued. Had he made his way across the stage into the motioning hands of the stagehand, the audience might have never noticed. But he didn't. He stayed. At home in the splendor. Roaming through the meadow of music.

He visited the woodwinds, turned his head at the trumpets, stepped between the flutists, and stopped by the side of the conductor. And Beethoven's Third Symphony came undone.

The musicians laughed. The audience laughed. The dog looked up at the conductor and panted. And the conductor lowered his baton.

The most historic orchestra in the world. One of the most moving pieces ever written. A night wrapped in glory, all brought to a stop by a wayward dog.

The chuckles ceased as the conductor turned. What fury might erupt? The audience grew quiet as the maestro faced them. What fuse had been lit? The polished German director looked at the crowd, looked down at the dog, then looked back at the people, raised his hands in a universal gesture…shrugged.

Everyone roared.

He stepped off the podium and scratched the dog behind the ears. The tail wagged again. The maestro spoke to the dog. He spoke German, but the dog seemed to understand. The two visited for a few seconds before the maestro took his new friend by the collar and led him off the stage. You'd have thought the dog was Pavarotti the way the people applauded. The conductor returned and the music began and Beethoven seemed none the worse for the whole experience.

Can you find you and me in this picture?

I can. Just call us Fido. And consider God the Maestro.

*If a dog will not come to you after having looked you in the face, you should go home and examine your conscience.*

WOODROW WILSON

And envision the moment when we will walk onto his stage. We won't deserve it. We will not have earned it. We may even surprise the musicians with our presence.

The music will be like none we've ever heard. We'll stroll among the angels and listen as they sing. We'll gaze at heaven's lights and gasp as they shine. And we'll walk next to the Maestro, stand by, and worship as he leads.

This chapter reminds us of that moment. It challenges us to see the unseen and live for that event. It invites us to tune our ears to the song of the skies and long—long, for the moment when we'll be at the Maestro's side.

He, too, will welcome. And he, too, will speak. But he will not lead us away. He will invite us to remain, forever his guests on his stage.

—MAX LUCADO

*When he sits before me*
*looking up, his eyes*
*shine like eager coals,*
*pleasing me his only desire.*

*My dog lies at my feet,*
*quiet now,*
*his eyes half closed,*
*taking restful breaths,*
*ready to rise and follow*
*where I go.*

*That I should know*
*my duty so well,*
*and follow where*
*my Lord calls me,*
*and hope in every word*
*from Him I hear.*

F. CALCINARI, JR.

Heaven goes by favour. If it went by merit,
you would stay out and your dog would go in.

MARK TWAIN

## Acknowledgments

"Things We Can Learn from a Dog" is from the July/August 1997 *Golden Retriever Journal*, p. 17.

"Only a Dog" is an epitaph from *Animal Heroes* by Byron G. Weis, Copyright © 1979 by Laurence Gadd. Used by permission from Macmillan Publishing Company.

"How to Talk to Your Dog" is adapted from *Why We Love the Dogs We Do* by Stanley Coren (New York: The Free Press, 1998), pp. 62-64.

"You Can Stay" is by Sue Monk Kidd, taken from *Dog Tales: Lessons in Love* from *Guideposts* (Carmel, NY: Dimensions for Living, 1995), pp. 16-17. Used by permission.

"What Do They Know That We Don't Know?" is adapted from *What Do Dogs Know?* by Stanley Coren and Janet Walker (New York: The Free Press, 1997), pp. 2-15.

"I'm Not Impressed" is adapted from Coren, *What Do Dogs Know?*, p. 91.

"Do You Hear What They Hear?" is adapted from Coren, *What Do Dogs Know?*, p. 24.

"Confessions Are Good for the Dog Owner" is adapted from Coren, *What Do Dogs Know?*, pp. 40, 42, 59, 86, 108, 110, and 112.

"The Book My Dog Has Always Wanted" is adapted from the back cover of *Heeling the Canine Within: A Dog's Self-Help Companion* by Max and Scooter (New York: Ballantine Books, 1998).

"Coming Home" is by David A. Redding, from *The Golden String*, Copyright © 1987 by David Redding. Used by permission from Fleming H. Revell Publishing Company.

"What's in a Name?" is adapted from Coren, *What Do Dogs Know?*, p. 106.

"The Guest of the Maestro" was told to Max Lucado by Erik Ketcherside. Max Lucado included it in his book *When God Whispers Your Name* (Dallas, TX: Word, Inc., 1994), pp. 166-68. Used by permission.

Harvest House Publishers has made every effort to trace the ownership of all poems and quotes. In the event of a question arising from the use of a poem or quote, we regret any error made and will be pleased to make the necessary correction in future editions of this book.

We never really own a dog as much as he owns us.

GENE HILL